SACRED TREES AND INDIAN LIFE

SACRED TREES AND INDIAN LIFE

PHOTOGRAPHS BY SUSANNE HAWKES

TEXT BY KARUNA GOSWAMY

Aryan Books International
New Delhi

Tree of Life and Knowledge; bronze, Vijaynagar period, 15th century

Sacred Trees and Indian Life

ISBN-81-7305-265-4

Published in 2004 by
ARYAN BOOKS INTERNATIONAL
Pooja Apartments, 4B, Ansari Road, New Delhi - 110 002 (INDIA)
Tel. : 2328 7589, 2325 5799; Fax : 91-11-2327 0385
E-mail : aryanbooks@vsnl.com

Illustrations:
on the dust-jacket: Small lengths of cloth brought as offerings and tied to the branches of a *peepal* tree in Sector 12, Chandigarh.
end-papers: A view of a single, giant banyan tree in village Cholti Kheri.

Layout and design by Kamal P. Jammual
Typeset in GoudyOldStyleBT 9/11pts
Computer Typeset at ABI Prints & Publishing Co., New Delhi
Printed in India at B.B.N. Printers, New Delhi

INTRODUCTION

This book is about the abiding bond that exists between trees and everyday life in India: especially between sacred trees and everyday life. This bond has always been there. As it subsists today, it may not be so easily visible, for one's attention is diverted by other things, and the air in any case is filled with too much noise, a surfeit of human greed. But the bond is there; this book is in fact an attempt to draw attention to its embedded existence.

As far as the past is concerned, the past to which our own day is linked through a fine network of ideas and impressions and memories, the existence of the bond comes across with far greater ease. Passage after luminous passage in early texts speaks of trees and their connection with life: not simply with life as it is lived, but with the very understanding of it. Take the following two passages, almost a random selection: one from the *Jatakamala*, a cycle of tales in which the former lives of the Buddha are told, and the other from one of the *Upanishads*, those mystical, esoteric texts in which some of the noblest thought of India is expressed.

The Buddhist tale goes under the name of the *Bhadda Sala Jataka*, the 'Tale of the Noble Sala Tree'. In it, "the Master", having just instructed "the Brethren" in the monastery about the true nature of the Great Being, speaks also of his deeds in a former birth. The story is long, but meaningful, and moving. And it is best told in words as close to the original as possible, for nothing else captures its flavour or its essence. "Once upon a time", it begins in a familiar fashion, and goes on to tell of a king, Brahmadatta, who wished to build for himself a palace unlike that of any other king in India: a structure supported by only one giant

column. The builders were summoned and told of the king's desire for such a magnificent palace. "Very good", they said, and away they went into the forest. "There they beheld many a tree, straight and great, worthy to be the single column of such a palace." But the difficulties of transporting such a tree along rough roads were enormous. With the king's consent, therefore, they started looking for a tree in the royal parks.

"The builders went to the park, and there they espied a lordly *sal* (*shorea robusta*) tree, straight and well grown, worshipped by village and town, and to it the royal family also were wont to pay tribute and worship; and they told the king. Said the king, 'In my park ye have found me a tree: good — go and cut it down'. 'So be it', said they, and repaired to the park, with their hands full of perfumed garlands and the like; then hanging upon it a five-spray garland, and encircling it with a string, fastening to it a nosegay of flowers, and kindling a lamp, they did worship, explaining, 'On the seventh day from now we shall cut down this tree: it is the king's command to cut it down. Let the deities who dwell in this tree go elsewhere, and not unto us be the blame.'

"The god who dwelt in the tree hearing this, thought to himself: 'These builders are determined to cut down this tree, and to destroy my place of dwelling. Now my life only lasts as long as this my abiding place. And all the young *sal* trees that stand around this, where dwell the deities my kinsfolk, and they are many, will be destroyed. My own destruction does not touch me so near as the destruction of my children: therefore I must protect their lives'. Accordingly at the hour of midnight, adorned in divine splendour, he entered into the magnificent chamber of the king, and filling the whole chamber with a bright radiance, stood weeping beside the king's pillow. At sight of him the king, overcome by terror, uttered the first stanza:

'Who are thou, standing high in air, with heavenly vesture swathed:/ Whence come thy fears, why flow the tears in which thine eyes are bathed?'

On hearing which the king of the gods (of the trees) repeated two stanzas:

'Within thy realm, O King, they know me as the Lucky Tree:/ For sixty thousand years I stood, and all have worshipped me.

Though many a town and house they made, and many a king's dwelling,/ Yet me they never did molest, to me no harm did bring:/ Then even as they did worship pay, so worship thou, O King!'

Then the king uttered two stanzas:

'But such another mighty trunk I never yet did see,/ So fine a kind in girth and height, so thick and strong a tree.

A lovely palace I will build, one column for support:/ There I will place thee to abide; thy life shall not be short.'

On hearing this, the king of the gods (of the trees) uttered two stanzas:

'Since thou art bent to tear my body from me, cut me small,/ And cut me piecemeal limb from limb, O King, or not at all.

Cut first the top, the middle next, then last the root of me:/ And if thou cut me so, O King, death will not painful be.'

Then the King repeated two stanzas:

'First hands and feet, then nose and ears, while yet the victim lives,/ And last of all the head let fall, a painful death this gives.

O Lucky Tree! O woodland king! What pleasure couldst thou feel,/ Why, for what reason, dost thou wish to be cut up piecemeal?'

Then the Auspicious Tree answered by repeating two stanzas:

'The reason (and a reason 'tis full noble) why piecemeal I would be cut, O mighty king! Come listen while I tell./ My kith and kin all prospering round me well-sheltered grow:/ These I should crush by one huge fall,—and great would be their woe.'

The king, hearing this was much pleased: 'Tis a worthy god this', he said, ' he does not wish that his kinsfolk should lose their dwelling place because he loses his; he acts for his kinfolk's good.' And he repeated the remaining stanza:

'O Lucky Tree! O woodland king! Thy thoughts must noble be:/ Thou wouldst befriend thy kindred, so from fear I set thee free.'

The king of the gods (of trees), having discoursed to this king, then departed. And the king being established according to his admonition, gave gifts and did other good deeds, till he went to fill the hosts of heaven."

The magical tale is filled with themes of ambition, kindness, the immanence of life, compassion, self-sacrifice, contrition. The other passage, however-from the *Chhandogya Upanishad*-has an altogether different flavour. As his Teacher, the sage Uddalaka Aruni is instructing his son, Shvetaketu, in the secrets of immanent reality, using parables and similes. One can imagine the two seated under a banyan tree in the hermitage, Shvetaketu looking up at his Teacher.

" 'Bring hither a fig from there.'

'Here it is, sir.'

'Divide it.'

'It is divided, sir.'

'What do you see there?'

'These rather fine seeds, sir.'

'Of these, please divide one.'

'It is divided, sir.'

'What do you see there?'

'Nothing at all, sir.'

Then he (the Teacher) said to him: 'Verily, my dear, that finest essence which you do not perceive: verily, my dear, from that finest essence this great *nyagrodha* (sacred fig, *ficus indica* or *ficus bengalensis*) tree thus arises.'

'Believe me, my dear', said he, 'that which is the finest essence, this whole world has that as its soul. That is Reality. That is *atman* (Soul). That art thou, Shvetaketu'."

Few, one can imagine, would be thinking thoughts such as this today. But the idea that there is a certain sacredness that inheres in trees, and there is much to learn from them, continues to survive. Thoughts might have yielded place to ritual today, and understanding replaced by simple, received belief. But, embedded somewhere, at some level, is the thought that a *vriksha*, literally that which 'grows', or 'breathes', is a *devata*, deity. One is reminded of this in so many ways.

I recall many occasions when passers-by, walking on the road along the outer wall of the garden of our home in Chandigarh, would suddenly stop to gaze at the luxuriant spread of a *bel* tree (*aeglos marmelosa*) that grew there. This tree is believed to be especially dear to Shiva, the great reclusive God, but not too many of them grow in this region. It is not a particularly attractive tree but, because of its association with Shiva, it is eminently sacred. Evidently these passers-by were simply taking in the sight of the tree, thoughts and auspicious associations crowding their minds. The *bel* trees bear rich fruit, hard on the outside but fleshy and sweet inside, that many savour as a delicacy, or use for medicinal purposes. But I recall being asked by some of them, total strangers, especially around Shivaratri time when Shiva's phallic emblem is worshipped with offerings of *bel* leaves, if they could pluck some leaves from our tree. When allowed, some bowed to the tree and others spent a long time searching out twigs which had clusters of five leaves – usually there are only three – since offering these brings great merit. I know that some of them found them.

Again, travelling from Chandigarh by train, one sees each time, very close to the railway track as one nears Delhi, a long and solidly built masonry wall, rising high, beyond which are some simple residential quarters. The wall, however, instead of looking plain, is dotted with clumps of roots and leaves of *peepal* trees (*ficus religiosa*) which seem to have forced their way, over a period of decades, through the cracks and crevices in the wall. No full-grown trees are in sight at this place although the place must certainly have been cleared of some trees that grew there before construction began. But the roots did obviously refuse to die, and they can be seen now, oddly shaped but covered with clusters of leaves, dotting the enormous, high wall, peeping out, surrealistic fashion. Almost certainly those residing in the buildings do not routinely see them, and the wall, being high and very close to the railway track, is not easy to approach from the outside. But, on occasions, with delighted eyes, I have seen, as the train begins to slow down in its approach, a flower garland suspended from some root or stumpy branch. Placed there by some unknown, but devout, hand.

This book, essentially a photographic essay, is about sights like these, and about the wonderful ways in which quietly, almost unobserved, ordinary lives continue to be touched by trees even in our own day. Most of the photographs were taken in and around Chandigarh. This was done with a clear intent, for Chandigarh is, arguably, the most 'modern', at least among the youngest, of Indian cities. But even here, in an urban, metropolitan setting, we discovered that a certain feeling for trees lives on. One speaks here not simply of things and sights that are evident and greet the eyes everywhere: trades carried on and congregations assembled, even whole lives lived under trees. One speaks of a certain reverence, and of finer feelings.

Much of it is not immediately apparent, and a certain opaqueness hides things from view. But the moment one starts looking, with clear eyes, one begins to see. What we uncovered, in the course of our search for the meaning that trees held for people, was remarkable. Once we started observing, and made our intent known to people that we knew, almost every day someone or the other came up and shared his or her thoughts with us, pointing out trees that were special, offering suggestions about going to see them at some especially appropriate hour or day. One day someone would speak of a spot where a *neem* and a *peepal* were growing, joined together and intertwined; the next day, a tree to which people resorted for the fulfilment of their wishes would be pointed out to us. Some informant or friend of the family would tell us to come and photograph their tree on a special day, for that is when all the women of the place bring to it food and other offerings; someone would call and invite us to go to the site where the *tulasi* plant (*ocimum sanctum*) is ritually 'married' to a *shaligrama*-ammonite which is the emblem of the great God, Vishnu. News of an enormous banyan tree which spreads over several hectares of land would be excitedly brought in, or someone would remind us that several life-sized figures of sages and holy men, cast in concrete, could be seen under another tree in the midst of a thickly populated sector of the town. Deliberately, we did not set out to record any 'spectacular' trees, nor were trees traditionally held sacred our only focus. We simply wished to get into the world of trees as perceived by people around us in Chandigarh. But even with this limited aim and focus, we discovered all manner of things, and recorded them. This we did with a mixture of delight and gratitude. The saffron or turmeric *tilak* applied to some branch, the threads wound around the trunk, the shrine hurriedly set up under a tree by a wandering *sadhu*, a solitary flower placed close to shrivelled roots, are all images that have stayed with us. For, through them, we found ourselves reaching out to a whole range of thoughts and feelings about trees that have always been a part of India.

K.G.

May plants, the waters and the sky
Preserve us, and woods
And mountains, with their trees for tresses ...

—Rigveda

A PERSONAL NOTE

Whenever I come to India, I am overwhelmed by the intensity with which this ancient land opens itself to me and captures all my senses.

I dive deep into the adventure of taste and smell that India offers: delightful and provocative at the same time, a curious mix of pervasive noise and profound silence, of experience and observation. What I partake of is a kind of visual ecstasy, which challenges, even as it fascinates, me.

The project that my friend, Karuna, and I started working on some two years ago, searching for the sacredness of trees, turned gradually into a pilgrimage, the exploration of another dimension of India.

Unlike back at home, in Europe, where trees have become very removed from their initial identity, tamed and enslaved by man as they are, of little service to man, neither humble nor obedient, in India the trees we often encountered were sacred, dwelling places of the godhead, still retaining their proud, self-assertive, 'tree-ness'.

Even in the middle of the hustle and bustle of a modern, earthy town, in the midst of all the noise and traffic, we discovered trees that are still ancient and grand, worshipped by men who approach them with devotion and veneration. At their feet they place devotional objects, *lingams*, sculptures, oblations, images of the Gods, and they tie threads around them and offer flowers, sweets, water and fire. In the courtyard of a temple we discovered a *tulasi* that had been adorned with a rose, had been garlanded and dressed in a precious garment.

The idea having taken 'possession' of us, as it were, we searched for trees like these, and found them everywhere that we travelled. From morning

until late in the afternoon, we kept looking, our quest keeping us going as we moved out of the town of Chandigarh and into the vast landscape of the Punjab. We landed upon sacred trees in temple yards, in the backyards of private homes, and in remote villages lying off the beaten track and approached only through dried out river-beds. As we found, a banyan or a *peepal* tree could be receiving worship and at the same time be the place for a homestead or a workshop for someone, or simply serve as a dwelling place of a *sadhu*. A visit to Nek Chand's tree sculptures in the Rock Garden in Chandigarh turned out to be another experience. Although these trees are art objects and are not sacred, they opened up yet another dimension of tree-consciousness to me. I can still close my eyes and recall their concrete-nakedness and boldness: no bark, no leaves, only coarse, aggressive trunk and stems, trees stripped to their bones, reminding one of petrified prehistoric plants and mammals. These 'trees' of Nek Chand appeared to me to be symbols of an essentiality which has transcended reality and yet preserves the core of its tree-identity.

We attended a moving, sacred ceremony in a village in the Punjab, where women were gathering to circle a huge *peepal* tree, for placing their devotional offerings at its foot. And at yet another location, in a temple that was bustling with hundreds of pilgrims, we saw a quiet ceremony being performed: tree-rituals of sacrifice and devotion.

For me, trees treated in this manner, with devotion and adoration, become holy. Or is it the other way around? The tree inhabited by the godhead is itself meditating, trance-bound still, remembering its sacred status from times immemorial, when the first tree sprang from a seed in the surge of creation. This mythical dimension can still be felt and observed. In and out of time, these trees remain what they ever were. Here are trees that have never been subjugated. We can find them in the heart of the modern city of Chandigarh and deep in the heart of the surrounding Punjab, or also elsewhere in India, expressing once again another aspect of man's hunger for transcendence and for his striving for the perception of the Divine in this matter-of-fact world.

Each tree that we visited was a feast to my eyes. Trees presented themselves to me with the consciousness of unique beings; they were self-contained and through them ran some kind of a majestic beauty, and nobility. And I was deeply impressed. Even in the photographs that I took, the dramatic incarnation of these trees, their solemn dignity, is very often manifest.

Lynceus, the tower warden, in Johann Wolfgang Goethe's *Faust* exclaims:

"*You blessed eyes,*
What you saw everywhere,
It be as it may,
It was, oh, so fair!"

My feelings at the end of our project were those of gratitude for the chance of becoming acquainted with some of the ancient trees of India, which in their very own way are abodes of worship. I shall remember them as living witnesses of the breathtaking creativity of the Divine Spirit and the ability of man to respond and bow to it with veneration.

S.H.

The blessed Lord spoke thus:

It is said that the ashvattha *tree is undying,*
Its roots above and its branches below,
Its leaves the sacred chants of the Vedas,
Whoever knows this, he is the knower of the Vedas.

– The Bhagavad Gita

Peepal (*ficus religiosa*; Skt. *ashvattha*) tree, growing next to the temple built by the Rajas of Patiala, in the proximity of the Mansa Devi shrine, Mani Majra, Union Territory of Chandigarh.

Brahma said:

He who eats eight buds of ashoka *flowers on the eighth day of the moon's increase in the month of* Chaitra *(March-April),*
marked by the asterism Punarvasu,
shall suffer no untimely bereavement.

– Garuda Purana

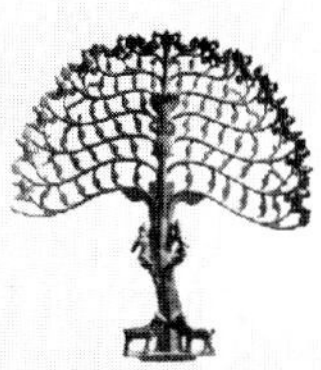

A row of *ashoka* (*saraca indica*) trees, growing along the precinct wall of the temple built by the Rajas of Patiala, in the proximity of the Mansa Devi shrine, Mani Majra, Union Territory of Chandigarh.

As the wide-spreading nyagrodha *tree is compressed in a small seed,*
so at the time of dissolution, the whole universe is comprehended
in Thee as its germ; as the nyagrodha *germinates from the seed,*
and becomes just a shoot and then rises into loftiness,
so the created world proceeds from Thee, and expands into magnitude.

– Vishnu Purana

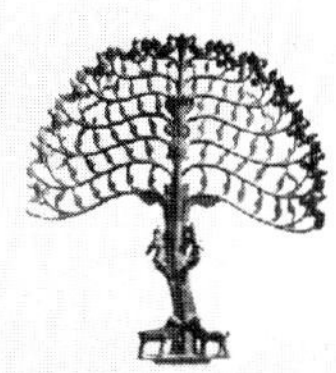

A giant banyan (*ficus bengalensis*; Skt. *nyagrodha*) tree growing in the village Cholti Kheri, on the Landran-Sirhind road in the Fatehgarh Sahib district of the Punjab. The aerial roots thrown by this ancient tree have by now turned into countless stems of their own, occupying a vast area, and they keep steadily encroaching upon the agricultural land around it. But, by common agreement, no one cuts or injures the tree.

The fig tree at this day to Indians known
In Malabar or Deccan, spreads her arms,
Branches so broad and long, that on the ground
The bended twigs take root, and daughters grow
About the mother tree, a pillar'd shade
High over-arched and echoing walks between.

– John Milton

Another view of the banyan tree in village Cholti Kheri on the Landran-Sirhind road. The tree also serves as a *dera* or resorting place for *Jogis*, followers of Shiva.

"What a noble place of worship!"

– Bishop Heber, on seeing a banyan tree

Another view of the banyan tree in village Cholti Kheri on the Landran-Sirhind road. Small shrines and sacred emblems are placed close to one section of its many 'trunks'.

There is only one place
For me to take shelter,
And that welcoming place
Is under my Lord's
Compassion – Smile – Tree.

– Sri Chinmoy

Banyan tree on the outskirts of the village Togan, Union Territory of Chandigarh. The hollows in the trunks of the tree serve as a shelter during the rains.

Brahma exists in its (the nyagrodha *tree's) roots;*
Vishnu in its trunk,
and Skanda in its branches.

– Vishnu Purana

Banyan tree in village Togan, Union Territory of Chandigarh.

A tree, when it is felled, grows up
From the root, more new again
A mortal, when cut down by death –
From what root does he grow up?

– Brihad Aranyaka Upanishad

Banyan tree on the way to village Togan, Union Territory of Chandigarh.

To whom shall I go to learn about
my Beloved?
Kabir says: 'As you never
may find the forest if you
ignore the tree, so he may never be found
in abstractions.'

Newly constructed brick temple under a banyan tree close to a bridge over a rivulet at Parwanoo, on the way to Shimla from Kalka.

'Please sir, tell me more of this teaching', said the boy.

'Very well, my son. If you were to chop at the root of this great tree, it would bleed but it would not die. If you were to chop at its trunk, it would bleed but it would not die. If you were to chop at the branches, it would bleed but it would not die. Permeated by sap, its life energy, the tree stands firm, drinking and enjoying its nourishment.

But if the sap withdraws from one of the branches then that branch withers. If it withdraws from a second branch then that branch withers. If it withdraws from a third branch then that branch also withers. If the sap withdraw from the whole tree then the whole tree withers and dies. In just the same way, my son, when the Self withdraws from the body the body dies, though the Self lives on.

And that being which is the subtlest essence of everything, the supreme reality, the Self of all that exists, THAT ART THOU, Shvetaketu.'

– The Chhandogya Upanishad

Mango tree in a park in Sector 9, Chandigarh.

The Lord said:

Of all the trees, I am the ashvattha
Of heavenly sages, Narada,
Of heavenly musicians, the foremost,
Of the perfected ones, the sage Kapila.

– The Bhagavad Gita

Peepal (*ficus religiosa*; Skt. *ashvattha*) tree on the outskirts of village Sarangpur, Union Territory of Chandigarh.

The birth of the trees is verily the most blessed in the world, as it contributes to the well-being of all creatures. Just as no needy person returns disappointed from benevolent persons, so is the case with a person who approaches these for shelter.

They (the trees) fulfil the desires of others by means of their leaves, flowers, fruits, shade, roots, bark, wood, fragrance, gums or exudations, ashes, coals and tender leaves.

– Bhagavata Purana

A cluster of bamboo trees: Leisure valley park, Sector 3, Chandigarh.

As soon as men look with pleasure at actual details of nature,
their symbolizing habit of mind gives to their regard an unusual intensity,
for they look at flowers and trees not only as delightful objects,
but as prototypes of the divine.

– Kenneth Clark

Bamboo trees: Leisure valley park, Sector 3, Chandigarh.

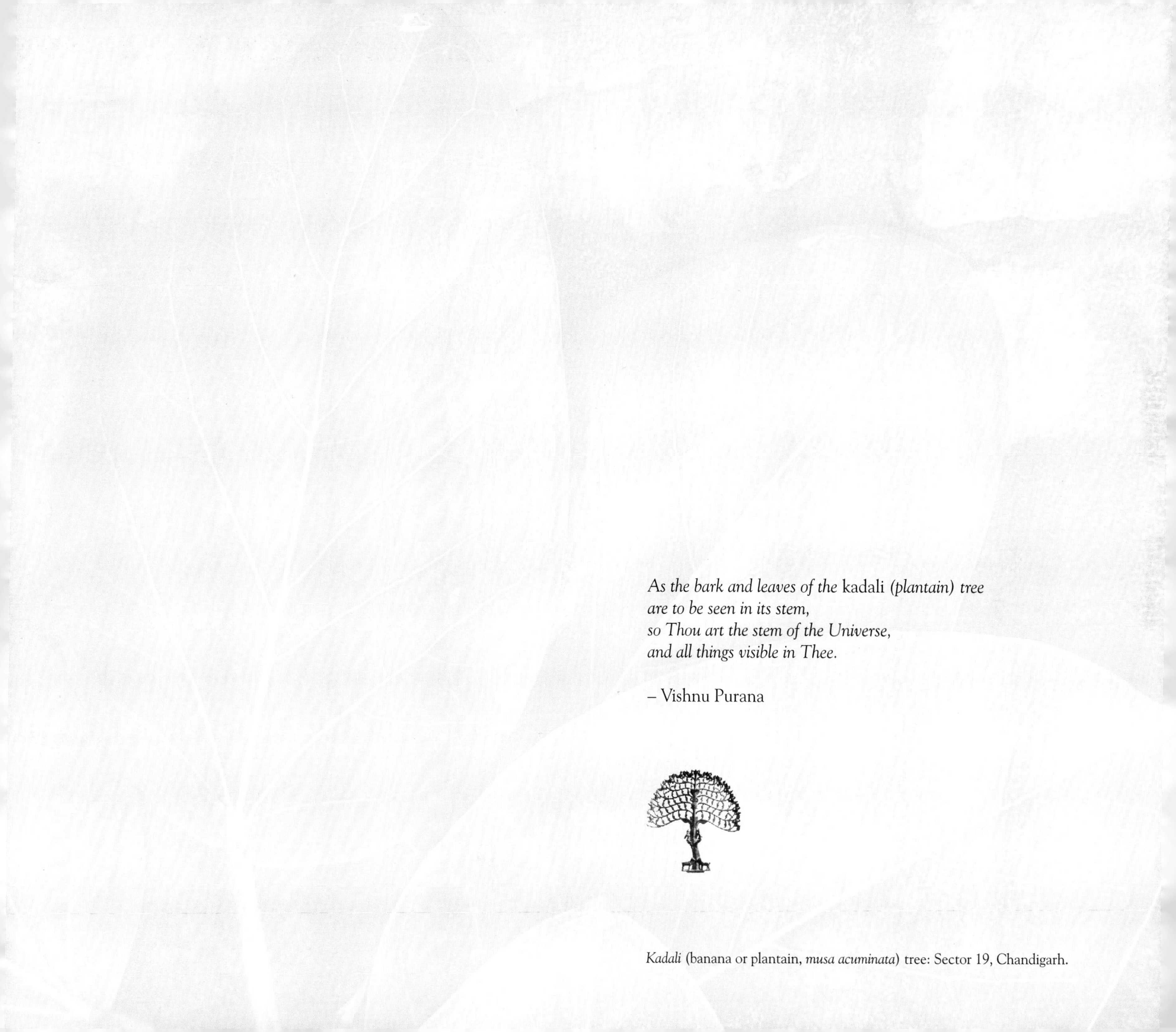

As the bark and leaves of the kadali *(plantain) tree*
are to be seen in its stem,
so Thou art the stem of the Universe,
and all things visible in Thee.

– Vishnu Purana

Kadali (banana or plantain, *musa acuminata*) tree: Sector 19, Chandigarh.

Growing Together

A *tulasi* (*ocimum sanctum*) and a vinca plant: compound of the Punjab Engineering College, Chandigarh.

"O mother tulasi, *who causes happiness to the heart of* Govinda*!*
I collect you for puja in the service of Narayana.
Obeisance to you! Keshava has no happiness without you.
Without you, O blissful one, deeds are without fruit."

– Kriyayogasara

Decorated and dressed up *tulasi* plant: Gaudiya Math, Sector 20, Chandigarh.

There is a strange tree, which stands
without roots and bears fruits
without blossoming; ....
Only two birds sing there; one is the
Guru, the other the disciple.

– Kabir

Concrete trees: Nek Chand's Rock Garden, Chandigarh.

Perceiving that the trees served as umbrellas by spreading their shade in the scorching heat of the summer sun,
Krishna addressed to his cowherd friends, the residents of Vraja:

Have a look at these great blessed souls who live only for the welfare of others, and themselves undergo (for others) the severity of stormy winds, heavy showers, summer heat and snow, and save them off from us.

– Bhagavata Purana

A new temple built under a tree, on the site of an older 10th century temple: village Mirzapur, Union Territory of Chandigarh.

A Gathering Place

Small sculptures and fragments of the old 10th century temple placed at the foot of the tree: village Mirzapur.

Reminders

Amalaka and other sculptural and architectural fragments placed at the foot of the tree: village Mirzapur, Union Territory of Chandigarh.

To Earth, hail!
On this choicest glory of God
Let us meditate.
May sweet be the atmosphere of the earth,
The trees be full of sweetness for us ...

– Brihad Aranyaka Upanishad

Banyan tree on the outskirts of the temple built by the Rajas of Patiala, near the Mansa Devi temple, Mani Majra, Union Territory of Chandigarh.

बालक नाथ
मंदिर

Waving in Homage

A cluster of banana trees at the shrine of Baba Balak Nath, near Mansa Devi temple on the outskirts of Chandigarh.

"To this parched forest, [with lamps],
their way the travellers made,
And spied a mighty banyan tree
with cool and pleasant shade ...."

– Maha-Vanija Jataka

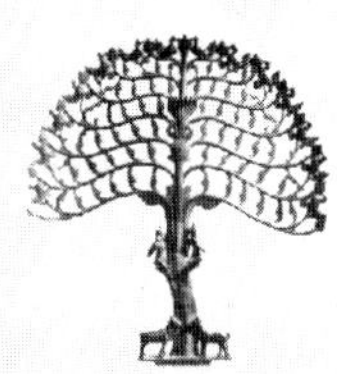

A little niche for burning incense and lighting lamps at the foot of a banyan tree in the compound of the Punjab Engineering College, Chandigarh.

"The merit of this gift, Sir, [said the followers of the Master], we renounce in favour of a tree-deity who gave us the whole treasure."

– Maha-Vanija Jataka

Ornamental veils in gold and red tied to the branches of a *peepal* tree in token of vows made or fulfilled: compound of the Mansa Devi temple, on the outskirts of Chandigarh.

Having brought to the tree
"the robes of many hues,
jewels and rings in plenty!",
the merchants all together stood beneath the leafy shade ....

– Maha-Vanija Jataka

Veils tied to the branches of the *peepal* tree in token of vows made or fulfilled, and a receptacle for offerings: compound of the Mansa Devi temple, on the outskirts of Chandigarh.

Simple Offerings

Small lengths of cloth brought as offerings and tied to the branches of a *peepal* tree in the compound of the Punjab Engineering College, Chandigarh.

"O ashvattha *tree! your roots represent Brahma, the Creator, your trunk represents Shiva, the Destroyer, and your branches, Vishnu, the Preserver. As such you are the emblem of* Trimurti. *All those who honour you in this world by performing* upanayana, *walk around you, adore you and sing your praises, obtain remission of their sins in this world and bliss in the next."*

– Vedic prayer, cited in Ragozin, Vedic India

Detail of offerings brought to the *peepal* tree and placed high in its branches: Mansa Devi temple, on the outskirts of Chandigarh.

Daily Offerings

Peepal tree in the compound of the Mansa Devi temple, on the outskirts of Chandigarh.

Sacred water brought to the tree.

Kavad, containers of water brought from the Ganga by *kavadias*, devotees of Shiva, and placed within the branches of the *peepal* tree at the Mansa Devi temple, on the outskirts of Chandigarh.

Rituals and Images

Sacred threads tied around the trunk of a *peepal* tree in the compound of a temple in Sector 24, Chandigarh.

Offerings

Small offerings, including fragmented images, and sacred threads: *peepal* tree in the compound of a temple in Sector 24, Chandigarh.

Threads and Flowers

Around a *peepal* tree in the compound of a temple in Sector 24, Chandigarh.

Anointing marks, rakhis *and other sacred threads.*

Peepal tree in the compound of the temple of the *nagara devata* at Mani Majra, on the outskirts of Chandigarh.

Reflections

Peepal tree growing in one corner of a small *baoli* or step-well at Pinjore on the Chandigarh-Kalka road.

The Lord said:

"A leaf, a flower, or fruit or water, that he offers with devotion
I take from the man of self-restraint in response to his devotion ...."

– The Bhagavad Gita

Peepal tree at Kalka, on the Chandigarh-Shimla Highway.

"The spirits which reside here,
the yatudhanas, guhyakas, *etc. all of them*
I offer worship and beg pardon of them, ...
Be pleased in every respect with these our offerings."

– Vanayagavidhi

The branches and roots of a tree, anointed with *haridra* (turmeric) powder, in the compound of a shrine of the *grama devata* [village deity] at Mani Majra, on the outskirts of Chandigarh.

Speaking of Shiva

A *trishul* or trident, emblem of Shiva planted at the foot of a tree and floral offerings: compound of the Chandigarh College of Architecture, Sector 12, Chandigarh.

Incense at the Altar

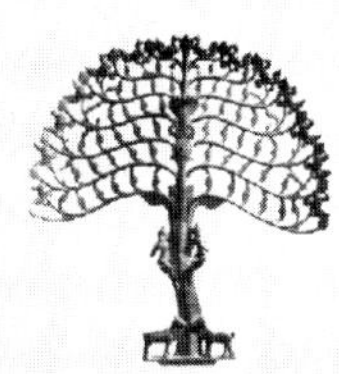

A make-shift incense burner at the foot of a tree: compound of the new temple, Sector 24, Chandigarh.

Worship with flowers and untwisted yarn-threads.

Garlands, etc., placed upon a freshly cut trunk of a banana tree: temple of the *grama devata* at Mani Majra, on the outskirts of Chandigarh.

Renewal Hopes

Offerings brought to a drying up *tulasi* plant: Lakshmi-Narayan temple, Sector 20, Chandigarh.

Reminders

Empty and discarded earthen pots from earlier rituals, left at the *thaan* (Skt. *sthana*): at the foot of the *peepal* tree on the outskirts of village Sarangpur, Union Territory of Chandigarh.

In remembrance of the departed.

Small brick structures, emblematic of and dedicated to ancestors, in regular worship at the *thaan*: village Sarangpur, Union Territory of Chandigarh.

Family Rituals

Women and children from different families offering water and food at the *thaan*: village Sarangpur, Union Territory of Chandigarh.

Homage and Remembrance

Grains and cooked food brought to miniature brick structures raised in honour of the departed, at the foot of the tree at the *thaan*: village Sarangpur, Union Territory of Chandigarh.

Recalling Past Memories

A woman pouring water over a sheet strewn with leaves and flowers placed at the foot of a *kikar* (acacia) tree that is held in special reverence by the family: village Sarangpur, Union Territory of Chandigarh.

A Special Offering

Traditional offerings of cowdung cakes to the *kikar* (acacia) tree on a day sacred to Sitala Mata, the 'goddess of smallpox': Mani Majra, on the outskirts of Chandigarh.

"O Bilva tree! Most prosperous, always a favourite of Shankara …."

– Prayer uttered on the occasion of the Durga Puja

Devotees pouring milk over, and offering leaves of the *bel* or *bilva* tree to, a '*shivalinga*', aniconic symbol of Shiva: the Shiva temple at Saketri, on the outskirts of Chandigarh.

Shelters: present and future.

Bricks and other construction material piled under a banyan tree: village Togan, Union Territory of Chandigarh.

As Life Moves On

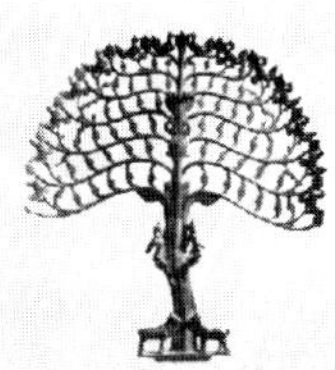

A barber at work in his 'establishment' under a tree: residential area, Sector 19, Chandigarh.

Life Cycles

A bicycle repair shed under a banyan tree: residential area, Sector 19, Chandigarh.

All that Sustains

A wanderer helping himself to a drink under a tree: Mansa Devi temple, on the outskirts of Chandigarh.

Nurturing the Sacred

A collection of vessels used for bringing water for pouring at the roots of a tree, and bathing miniature *shivalingas*: the compound of a temple, Sector 23, Chandigarh.

A Summoning of Energies

Icons of different descriptions placed at the foot of a tree: compound of a temple in Sector 24, Chandigarh.

The Protector and the Protected

A concrete image of the fearsome deity, Bhairon, placed under a tree, and some children from the neighbourhood: compound of the Government College for Men, Sector 11, Chandigarh.

Vrikshavasa: *an ascetic, one who lives in the hollow of a tree.*

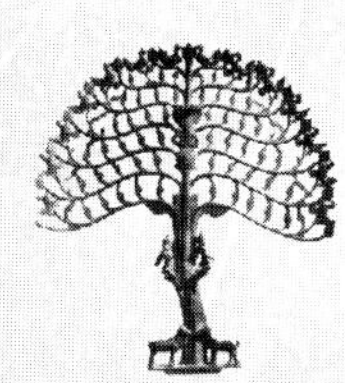

An image in concrete of an ascetic, made by Nek Chand for placing under a tree: Sector 24, Chandigarh.

"Lords of the Forest! Grant us life, strength, glory, splendour, offspring, cattle, abundant wealth, virtue, knowledge, intelligence …."

– Prayer commonly uttered at dawn

A group of figures in concrete, made by Nek Chand: Sector 24, Chandigarh.

A Gathering of Sages

A group of figures in concrete, made by Nek Chand: Sector 24, Chandigarh.

A Humble Offering

A *peepal* (*ficus religiosa*) leaf, placed at the foot of a stone image of Krishna playing upon the flute: Sector 19, Chandigarh.

Drenched in Light

A sprig of leaves hugging the side of a stone sculpture: Sector 19, Chandigarh.

It is on a single leaf of the nyagrodha *tree* (ficus bengalensis) *that Vishnu sleeps during the great deluge at the end of an aeon.*
It is there that the sage Markandeya found him as he looked for him in the waters of eternity.

– The Puranic Index

Leaves of a banyan (*ficus bengalensis*) tree.

Where neem *lives, sickness dies*

– Popular saying

Leaves from a *neem* (*margosa*) tree.

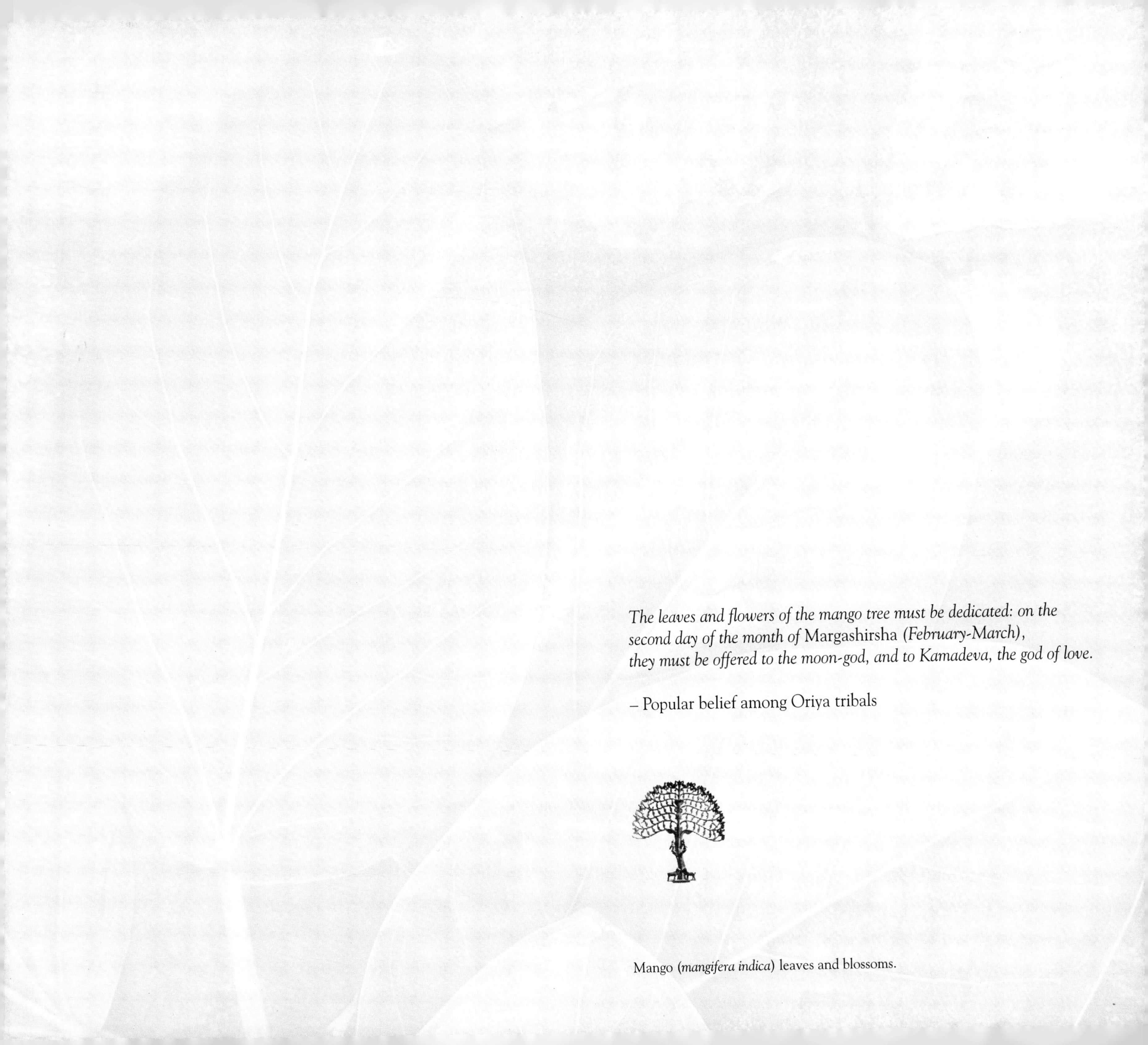

The leaves and flowers of the mango tree must be dedicated: on the second day of the month of Margashirsha *(February-March), they must be offered to the moon-god, and to Kamadeva, the god of love.*

– Popular belief among Oriya tribals

Mango (*mangifera indica*) leaves and blossoms.